THE MISADVENTURES

OF

SUZIE HOMEMAKER

by

Suzanne A. Fridenmaker

ISBN 978-1-62747-049-0
eISBN 978-1-62747-050-6

Table of Contents

In memory of my mother-in-law
Bonnie Jean Fridenmaker,
who has been in heaven for over
thirty years.
I quickly grew to love her,
but had so little time
to learn her tips, recipes,
and tremendously gracious
hospitality.
With undying love to my husband,
daughter, and son
who inspire me.
Also, gratitude to my best friend who
encourages me in my journey.

Proverbs 31:10–31

King James Version

"Who can find a virtuous woman?
for her price is far above rubies.

The heart of her husband doth safely trust in her,
so that he shall have no need of spoil.

She will do him good and not evil all the days of her life.

She seeketh wool, and flax,
and worketh willingly with her hands.

She is like the merchants' ships;
she bringeth her food from afar.

She riseth also while it is yet night, and giveth
meat to her household, and a portion to her maidens.

She considereth a field, and buyeth it: with the fruit
of her hands she planteth a vineyard.

She girdeth her loins with strength,
and strengtheneth her arms.

She perceiveth that her merchandise is good:
her candle goeth not out by night.

She layeth her hands to the spindle,
and her hands hold the distaff.

She stretcheth out her hand to the poor;
yea, she reacheth forth her hands to the needy.

She is not afraid of the snow for her household:
for all her household are clothed with scarlet.

She maketh herself coverings of tapestry;
her clothing is silk and purple.

Her husband is known in the gates,
when he sitteth among the elders of the land.

She maketh fine linen, and selleth it;
and delivereth girdles unto the merchant.

Strength and honour are her clothing;
and she shall rejoice in time to come.

She openeth her mouth with wisdom;
and in her tongue is the law of kindness.

She looketh well to the ways of her household,
and eateth not the bread of idleness.

Her children arise up, and call her blessed;
her husband also, and he praiseth her.

Many daughters have done virtuously,
but thou excellest them all.

Favour is deceitful, and beauty is vain:
but a woman that feareth the LORD, she shall be praised.

Give her of the fruit of her hands;
and let her own works praise her in the gates."

Introduction

Are you struggling with the decision whether or not to be a stay-at-home mom? Maybe you are a homemaker raising children and wrestling with feelings of insecurity or lack of appreciation. Or perhaps you are a homemaker now toying with the idea of joining the workforce. As a former first-grade teacher, day-care worker for preschoolers, and district liaison teacher for teens in behavioral lockdown wards, I know the importance of providing stability in the home for a young developing child as well as a vulnerable adolescent.

I took a year-long maternity leave with our first child and never returned to full-time work outside the home. Believe me, there is more than full-time work IN the home, and the benefits package exceeded that of any other. Fortunately, I am blessed to have the emotional and financial support of my husband. However, I have found that there are plenty of opportunities for earning money, ways to save money, and avenues to help my children and my husband start their own businesses. I am a planner, but God has even better plans for us than I imagined.

As you read my story, I invite you to take time to step back, reflect, and evaluate, perhaps with pen in hand. This may help you to be open to God's leading in your life and to decide if "home is where your heart is." I pray that you will gain insight into your situation and a sense of direction for your future.

Home Is Where the Heart Is

by Suzanne A. Fridenmaker

"Home is where the heart is,"
As the saying goes;
What do those words mean,
Or is it just prose?

I believe it means
That your home life shows
What you value most:
From whence your love flows.

Start with a pure heart,
Then as your love grows,
Still protect your heart;
Keep it white as snow.

On your very home
Blessing will bestow;
A new love will bud
And bloom before you know.

First Impressions

Have you ever had the experience of going to an antique store and finding something that you remember from your grandparents' home? A fondness may well up in your heart. What about seeing something that you had in your own kitchen when you were growing up? A spark of remembrance may light up in your eyes. Maybe you have happened upon one of your childhood toys and a whole realm of glee overtakes you. A sense of awe and "ahs" brings you back to the place when all seemed right in a simpler world. I had that profound experience when I spied a childhood item. Allow me to share my impressions.

As a young girl, I remember being fascinated by my friend's Hasbro Easy Bake Oven. It was a conveyer oven much like the Quizno's ovens. I would watch the process of baking and expectantly wait for the pan to go through the cooling chamber. Finally, I got to see the finished product and marvel at how wonderful the cake came out. To have my own oven would have been the "frosting on the cake." For one exciting occasion, I got the perfect gift: the Suzy Homemaker Oven. What could be better than that? After all, my name was Suzie, and I dreamed of being a homemaker.

Oh, the fun of stirring the cake batter in the pink plastic bowl, and then pouring the mix into the small round metal pan. What anticipation I felt when waiting for it to come out of the oven! I found that "you could have your cake and eat it, too."

I loved my bright turquoise oven, and it seemed to change my life in a profound way. There was something tangible that gave me a sense of power and accomplishment, all under the guise of playing house and seeing myself as a future homemaker. How appropriate that my name was Suzanne Baker, always called Suzie at home. Very soon, my nickname became Suzie Homemaker.

I was not one to be encouraged to help in the kitchen, except with doing dishes or setting the table. I think I loved the idea of cooking and baking, because I loved Grandma Baker, who had been so terrific at it, and she had five girls. The oldest was a career woman—a charge nurse. Very impressive for those days. The next girl was a professionally trained vocalist who later suffered from silicosis, a lung disease. She did a lot of crocheting and crafts that she could do sitting down. The other three girls loved to bake. I loved watching my aunts bake. I loved the image of Miss Perfect Hostess wearing an apron in the kitchen like Mrs.

Cleaver, and then donning the fancy apron when it's time to serve afternoon tea to the ladies.

Later, I got a wonderful gift of the Suzy Homemaker Washer. I was thrilled to wash my dolly's clothes. Mind you, my doll Colleen was as tall and as big as some two-year-olds. Hence, the clothes were not Barbie-sized, but they fit so nicely in the tub of the top loader. I was so relieved that my washer could be in the den and not in the basement like my mom's laundry room.

I was fascinated by the ironing or pressing process. Don't ask me why. We had a play ironing board and iron either at home or at church. I enjoyed ironing Colleen's clothes.

Also, somewhere along the line, we had a small broom just my size. I swept our hardwood flooring and felt like a helper. It was fun until I had to use the dust mop to get the dust bunnies hiding under my bed. That scared me.

In elementary school, I joined the Brownies and then advanced to the Girl Scouts. We did jobs to earn badges. Some of my jobs were to iron real garments, cook real food, and even sew and mend real clothes. I remember ironing my daddy's white handkerchiefs and folding them "just so" for his dresser drawer. My daddy was a pastor, and he was always lending a clean hanky to a burdened church member he was counseling or to a repentant sinner at the altar.

My mommy was always the perfect hostess by entertaining people from the church, community, or mission field. She was so good that I wanted to someday be the mommy and hostess she was. In reality, she had to work very hard at fulfilling that role. I just thought it was a natural part of being the mommy and wife. I wanted to be the perfect homemaker. That woman was pictured in a bathtub on commercials saying, "Calgone, take me away!" I loved bubble baths. It was fun to make crazy hairdos in the tub or add a beard or mustache. Goodie—I could look forward to baths even as an adult.

Take a minute to recall your early impressions of homemaking.

What were your aspirations for your future home life?

The Bubble Bursts

Oh, to live in a fantasy world where everyone has the Midas touch. During your youth, you probably realized that you live in an imperfect world. That realization hits some people as hard as cement, while for others it lands softly on a load of folded towels as with Snuggle Bear on the commercial. Still others just get stuck and can't seem to move on. Here's my account of when my little bubble burst.

One time, I accidently let my cake bake too long in the Suzy Homemaker Oven. The sophisticated light-bulb heating element melted the inside door window. It was dual paned, just like the oven door windows of today. These panes, however, were made of plastic. Only the inside pane melted. I felt horrible. My perfect little oven was no longer perfect. That didn't stop me from using it, though.

What could go wrong with my perfect Suzy Homemaker Washer? The washer had a hose on the back to drain the water over the sink after the wash cycle. One time, I didn't attach the hose well enough in the "upright fastened position," and the water drained on our wood flooring and area rug in the den. That didn't stop me from using that appliance either. I loved being responsible for my doll's clothes, and I didn't have to be down in the scary basement laundry room to do it.

Being the third child in the family, I was the favorite recipient of my older siblings' teasing. One evening, when my mommy and daddy were gone and a sitter supposedly was watching us, my brother and sister dared me to go down the bathtub drain. I was old enough to know that it was impossible! Next, they dared me to flush myself down the toilet. I reasoned I was too big to go down the hole. They were not very smart.

Finally, they dared me to go down the clothes chute that originated in the upstairs bathroom and ended in the basement laundry room. Now, that seemed reasonable, because I could easily fit in the chute, so I accepted the dare. I decided to go feet-first. So far, so good. Suddenly, I was stuck with just my arms, neck, and head showing. I called for help. My brother and sister tried to pull me out and then to push me down the rest of the way. Now, the babysitter couldn't budge me at all. Back then, it wasn't always possible to reach people by phone. For hours, I hung there waiting for my strong daddy to come home and rescue me.

Years later, I wondered what would have happened if I had decided to go head-first. I certainly would have passed out if I'd gotten stuck. The other variable was wondering whether or not my brother and sister had moved the rolling basket downstairs to catch me or if my head would have cracked on the cement. All in all, it could have been worse, though it didn't feel like it at the time.

Thinking back to when Dad built our freestanding garage, he designed it with a long deep shelf that extended the full length of the far wall. Until he needed to use all that space, he let me put down carpet scraps on the shelf and then my two appliances, along with other special toys to make it feel homey. That is where I would play house with my best friend, Joanne. We even took a giant spool—which previously must have had utility cable on it, wrapped carpet on it, turned it on its side, and made it into a rocker. We took play dishes and other precious things up there to make it seem more real. How I loved "playing house."

I was fascinated also with sewing. My grandma Baker would sew at least one outfit or item for each of her twenty-three grandchildren. I remember the things she made for me and the excitement upon receiving them. How special I felt. The dress was made especially for me to fit me, and was so much nicer than hand-me-downs I often wore. Also, my aunt on my mom's side of the family sewed the special doll clothes for Colleen that I loved so much. Those were made especially for MY doll.

When a little older, someone gave me a little kit to make a Barbie outfit. Wow! It was great with the lines to show where to cut, hand stitch, and place the snaps. I thought I was something pretty special to make my own Barbie clothes.

Then I became old enough to knit with an empty wooden spool that had nails hammered on the top where the label had been. I made long snakelike chains fed through the hollow part of the spool. When the chain was long enough, I ended it and then sewed the chain together in a spiral to make a circular rug or into whatever shape I wanted.

In Girl Scouts, we learned to hand sew many types of stitches. My grandma Wellman taught me to hem. She tried to teach me to crochet, but it was like chess. It was too complicated for me to strain my brain. Instead, I enjoyed making potholders using colorful stretchy bands that I looped and wove on a loom. Now that was fun.

One of the household tasks I learned for a Girl Scout badge was how to defrost the freezer compartment of our refrigerator. I would boil a pan of water, set it in the open freezer, and see the glacier melt ever so slightly. As soon as the pan cooled, I would replace it with another pan that had been boiling and continue to switch them out. In between, I chiseled away at the layers of frosty ice till the iceberg finally melted and I saw the surface of the freezer. I threw out any frost-burned food; however, ice cream had to be consumed in its entirety.

I took home economics in junior high school. It was given as a swing class: an innovative concept of thirteen weeks focused on sewing and then thirteen weeks on cooking. Our class was held in the brand new wing just dedicated that year. Sewing with machines was all new and exciting for me. I was attentive but cautious. For the first two weeks, we sewed only paper. The teacher had drawn lines of different lengths to show different stitch lengths, then curvy ones, and eventually a complete spiral. It was as fun as my Hasbro Spirograph at home with which I loved to draw designs of different colors. This method of sewing on paper patterns really gave me a lot of confidence.

Now for our project: an apron that we would later use during the cooking phase of the class. The aprons weren't to be fancy things, just functional. Mine was made of a brown medium-weight cotton fabric. I used contrasting thread so that the stitches would show and the teacher could easily judge the efforts. I worked so hard to make mine perfect. Having no prior experience, I was nervous and proud at the same time. My ego was bruised when I got my grade back. It may have only been an A- or a B+, but to me it represented failure. She noted that I hadn't trimmed every hanging thread from where the stitches began or ended. How did I miss that with contrasting colors no less? I felt very low. Perfection was not easily attainable. I didn't pursue sewing for years.

What things or events have caused discouragement for you in your role as a homemaker?

Do you have feelings of inadequacy?

Cheerleading Squad

In school, did you experience a love/hate relationship with cheerleaders? Perhaps you wanted to "stack up" to their level but fell flat, so you chose the path of envy and disdain. Look beyond those hang-ups and see that cheerleaders in the "game of life" play an important role. They may be disguised in various forms, whether or not fitting of the stereotype.

I am thankful that I yielded to several cheerleaders in my life. My biggest fan who cheered me on was my dad. He could see beyond my shortcomings in junior high when I didn't "measure up."

The home ec. cooking class would be great. The new room had an island demonstration table with an overhead adjustable mirror, so that everyone could see well. I was so impressed. I learned that there was a difference between liquid and solid measurements. A whole new world opened up to me. But alas, the cooking class was scary, too. It seemed like a real chore instead of a fun activity. I backed off from cooking for a lot of years. Baking was a different story, though. It was always good if it involved sugar or chocolate.

Joanne, my childhood friend, had a grandmother from Italy who made pizzelles. Joanne taught me how to make them using an iron press, and then taught me how to make cream puffs. I became hooked on cream puffs, store-bought or homemade, but I only made them at Joanne's house.

My friend in junior high, Gayle, was a lot of fun. Her grandmother loved to cook, and her mom loved to give us new experiences. I had my first "taffy pull" at her house.

At ten years of age, I went to Pennsylvania to spend a week at Grandpap and Grandma Baker's home. Like her name, Grandma Baker was great in the kitchen. She was the family camp cook for years, in addition to raising a family of nine! At my age, I was interested in playing with my cousins, but I also marveled at my aunts' cooking. On a trip a few years later, it was dessert time at an aunt's house. We made hot fudge sauce to go over vanilla ice cream. She wanted ME to help HER! That was a first experience for me. I could hardly contain my excitement and pride and came home with a recipe card.

Sometimes, when visiting my grandparents, we would go over the border to Ohio, where they had a cabin at the family campgrounds. The cabin had an icebox.

Later on, they got a refrigerator, and the icebox became part of the décor on the back porch just feet away from the outhouse door.

I recall the baby shower our junior high youth group gals gave for our intern leaders. Gayle and I decided to host it. Because the interns' last name was Noah and their family was expanding, we decided to honor her by making the cake in the shape of Noah's Ark. Oh, the fun we had with imperfection. It was okay because we did it together, and I didn't care whether or not it was perfect. I didn't have to take full responsibility or receive a grade! That is when I first learned my all-time favorite trick of using toothpicks to support any unsteady pieces. You know, that works much better when you have a designated cake server who knows where the toothpicks are, so they don't spear anyone's mouth.

During my junior high years, Mom felt I was now old enough to begin my rotation of cleaning the bathroom. She was so good at somehow making it seem like a milestone or a real honor. At first, it was fun, and then after a few years, it seemed like it was always my turn. Hmmmm. One week, she asked if I ever cleaned the base of the toilet. *Why?* I thought. That is when my innocence was lost, and I learned that males don't necessarily use accurate aim. Ugh. It was never the same when cleaning a toilet.

One time in seventh-grade science class, I sat down in my assigned seat during first period. It was in the very back of the room, because my teacher knew I would pay attention even back there. I didn't look at my seat before sitting to notice that there was fiberglass on the chair. Of course, I moved it, but it was too late, as I was wearing a skirt. After fidgeting through the period, I had Dad pick me up and take me home. Then I took a soak in the tub to get some relief from the itching. The humiliation didn't go down the drain, so baths took on a bad association. Maybe that is when I started taking showers.

Around ninth grade, Dad really wanted me to learn to sew. He knew I could excel. Flashbacks of home ec. made me reluctant, but what was I to do when he bought a machine and it came with free lessons? I went with fear and trepidation to downtown Detroit for the classes. I came back with just enough less resistance so that when Dad suggested that a young bride in our church, whom I adored, could also show me the ropes, I consented. We made a dotted Swiss navy-and-white shift dress with a matching bag. The dots formed the pattern of little hearts. I proudly wore it to church, but I'm not sure I was confident enough to wear it to school.

During college, I sewed with an experienced seamstress in our church. We made a brown-and-tan muslin dress. It turned out okay, and I made the best of the experience. But I wasn't a real looker in it, let's just say. I kept trying. Another girl encouraged me, and I made an Ultrasuede dress, the scraps from which later came in handy.

Now, the real kicker. I needed a job, because my summer job had ended. Cloth World was hiring. I passed the entrance test, but the employees were supposed to wear apparel that they had made themselves. That meant more sewing; however, employees got a discount. I now shudder to think of my lack of experience when giving novice customers and seasoned seamstresses advice. That job only lasted about eight months, but it gave me a significant push.

Who has positively influenced you as a homemaker, wife, or mother?

Is there someone who could come alongside to help?

Yolking or Choking

As a young woman, were you eager to find your true love and get married? Did you willingly say "I do" only to choke back tears of "why did I" after the honeymoon was over? I was starry eyed like most brides, and then was stunned and seeing stars during the first few months of our marriage. (Literally, I was seeing spots and had to go off the birth control pill!) The Lord helped me to a place of equilibrium over the years. I'll begin before we were married.

My family was out of town while I stayed home one particular time. I wanted to impress my Wellman grandparents, so I had them over for a meatloaf dinner. I knew I could do it, though I never had before. Oh, my goodness, was it ever underdone? We didn't know about *E. coli* back then! Grandma showed graciousness that day like never before.

The next year, my boyfriend came to see me in California while I was attending college. I lived in an off-campus house with five other girls. Again, I wanted to impress, so I planned to prepare a meal for him when my roommates were away. I thawed hamburger the night before to make meatloaf, his favorite meal that his mom made. But I forgot to put the hamburger meat in the refrigerator before bed, and it sat on the counter overnight. I called a friend and asked for advice. With no car to get to the store quickly and being a poor college student, I was devastated. She assured me it would be fine, because the oven heat would kill the germs. I made very sure this meatloaf was baked all the way.

Microwaves introduced a newfangled method of cooking. Wow! I remember seeing them in friends' homes, but I had never used one before. We got one for Christmas. Mom didn't have a clue how to use one. Being of the younger generation, I wasn't afraid of new technology. Well, let me tell you, I know how to pulverize a pork chop—believe you me.

Fortunately, I did learn quickly from my microwave failures. I've only seen the glow and sparks from silverware and foil one time each. Recently, I heard that if one's phone battery dies, it can be nuked in the micro for a few seconds. Supposedly, it's like resuscitating the phone back to life with a defibrillator. "I know CPR!" I wasn't going to fall for that one.

In fact, I had firsthand experience with being resuscitated. As a young girl of four, I was so excited because my uncle, his wife, and my newborn cousin from out of town were coming to visit. In those days, you told your hosts what day you'd be coming and perhaps what time of day. But without cell phones, not much advance warning could easily be given. Mommy was finishing up her cleaning and had not yet put away the vacuum cleaner. I heard that they had arrived and ran with abandon to greet them. My foot caught on the cord of the old black-and-silver canister vacuum, and I passed out cold.

As a teenager, I thought we had moved up big time when we got a copper tone upright freezer for the outside storage room. It was complete with auto-defrost. I was sad when we had to sell it, because we were moving across country. When Mom asked if I would clean it up so that we could sell it for a good price, I was proud to take on the challenge and began using a scouring pad on the beautiful outside finish. What could be better than the cleaning method I had used on pots and pans? Horrors, I didn't know it would take off the finish! Even though it didn't sell for nearly as much as it would have, Mom was very forgiving.

I've had many interesting laundry room tales over the years. I went from the scary downstairs one that I avoided to a lovely main floor one, which also served as our dog's domain. I loved that room. Then in high school, when we moved, the laundry room was a sad place till we remodeled. Next came the house with the appliances hidden behind folding doors.

College brought more stories as the laundry room was directly across from my dorm room. That is when quarters became valuable. The tradeoff for the annoying noises so close by was a fridge where I could stash my goodies for those late-night study sessions.

I once took a summer job as a maid at a huge three-campus Christian campground in California. I cleaned hundreds of toilets in nice hotel-like rooms, cabins, and public meeting areas. One particular day, I had one of the cabin rotations. I had an information sheet telling which cabins were occupied that week and needed to be cleaned. Whether it was their error or mine, I cleaned a particular cabin that day. I thought it strange that they had so much stuff for just one week. And the toilet was disgusting. I had never seen anything like it before. Days later, an embarrassed summer employee thanked me for cleaning her cabin. She and her husband had a horrible virus and had gone to see the camp nurse while I was cleaning their toilet for them. Ugh! I believe that accounted for my subsequent stomach bug.

One of the perks of working at the camp was to hear well-known and even famous orators over the loud speakers as you cleaned. After work, we would sit in on the meetings and concerts. The next fall, along with thousands of people, I attended a church to hear one of those well-known speakers. It was enthralling. I waited to meet him after the service. I was ecstatic yet nervous to meet him and promptly told him that I had cleaned his toilet. Impressively smooth move.

At this camp, the maids shared a work station with two really cute laundry boys, along with handsome and funny maintenance guys. We were all young college students. The laundry machines for the camp were huge, but we did our personal laundry at the posh dorms where we stayed. The laundry room was common ground for the guys and girls who otherwise had separate dorms. A quarter got you a cheap date, and laundry took on a whole new meaning that summer.

The next year of college, when I moved to off-campus housing, I had to walk to the Laundromat blocks away. I tried not to get my clothes dirty that semester.

The next year, I transferred to a university and was living "back home" in a state where my family had since moved. One Sunday, I wanted to look extra special for church when seeing my boyfriend (the meatloaf boyfriend just so happened to live in the same town and attended the same church). I decided to wear my memorable high school homecoming dress.

Noticing that the lace collar was wrinkled, I decided that a nice HOT IRON would take care of that. It sure did…good-bye to an even more memorable dress.

My soon-to-be mother-in-law Bonnie (yes, her son was the meatloaf boyfriend) gave me a birthday gift in college. It was a pattern, thread, and fabric to make a dress. I was no longer getting discounts or incentives to sew from the store. It was a much nicer fabric and a more fashionable pattern than I ever had. I made the springtime-like dress and wore it with pride and gratitude. The fabric never needed ironing.

When my aunt was in town for my wedding, she asked if my gown needed pressing. My $400 satin-and-lace dress (four times as expensive as the average bride spent in those days) had been in a dress bag for a couple of weeks hanging at the neighbor's house. It had been hiding there so that my snoopy fiancé wouldn't take a peek before the ceremony. My aunt spent hours pressing it, but she didn't melt any of it! In fact, a month later, she traveled to another state for my sister's wedding and did the same for her. Years later, she traveled to a third state for the third sister's gown. I still don't know why I couldn't have saved my aunt the trouble and done the ironing myself.

Grandma Wellman wanted to crochet an afghan for our wedding gift. She had us pick our colors and pattern. I

remember shopping with her at Woolworths for the yarn.
I have rarely regretted asking my husband's advice, but
you see, he was the ultimate involved groom. He had a
say in practically everything for our wedding and
registry. I thought it romantic for him to care so much.
When asked, he wanted an afghan that would cover our
queen-sized bed from top to bottom and hang all the way
down the sides of the bed. Grandma was puzzled by our
request, questioned me, but sweetly complied, working
on it for months on end! Once finished, it was so heavy
that I could hardly carry it by myself. The weight of the
yarn hanging off the bed over time made it so clumsy to
use. It has been in a box in storage for years and years.
Thankfully, my husband has grown wiser and always
listens to me. Uh…I mean to say that now I can always
trust his judgment.

Organization is the key to any successful household. I
love the thought of everything being in perfect order. My
mother and father were into "everything has a place,"
although they each had their own "don't touch zone."

I thought myself to be an orderly person, yet when I
married my husband, I suddenly felt like Oscar of *The
Odd Couple*. I tried my best to keep things tidy, but I
have a way of spreading out my many current projects
over many rooms. What's the problem with that? I soon

learned. I can remember a time when I had a complete inventory of everything in our home, except for the box upon box of childhood memorabilia in storage.

Paul instructs in Colossians 3:18 (New International Version), "Wives, submit to your husbands, as is fitting in the Lord." As a teenager, I was taught that the husband was the umbrella over the wife. I pictured the umbrella as something trapping me and stunting my growth. Now I see the umbrella as a welcome shelter that travels with me and expands as needed. I respect my husband and flourish with the knowledge that I am loved and protected.

How do you perceive your relationship with your husband?

Do you feel trapped or protected?

Communication Gap

Communication breakdowns happen to all of us. There used to be some valid reasons for gaps before technology linked us together. Today, with all of our conveniences, we don't have as many convenient excuses.

Sometimes the breakdowns are caused by our perceptions that don't allow us to listen as we should. Other times we don't speak up when we should. Thankfully, sometimes we keep silent. I've had my share of gaps in communication, and I'm glad I kept silent a few times as well.

The Baker aunt who was the vocalist didn't ask what kind of afghan we wanted for our wedding, and she already knew our colors. She made a lap-sized afghan that we have used and used and will continue to use while thinking of her in heaven.

My future husband and I went over to his sister's house where they had a young boy and a toddler boy at the time. They had an olive green suede couch to go with their Mediterranean décor. Sandy cautioned me where not to sit because of some spilled formula. I thought to myself, *Hmmm…what kind of a mother is she?* Then another time, we found a missing banana between the back cushions of the same couch. I tried not to show my horror.

Cooking was a struggle for the first years of our marriage, as my husband was a better cook than I was. He was kind and I learned...at least we didn't starve. I also found that I had a new standard to live up to: my new mother-in-law. Even though I adored her, I so wanted to instantly be as terrific as Bonnie in every way. Hmmm...I wonder what she had been like as a newlywed.

My husband started out our marriage as a floor nurse at the hospital. I would get so upset when he would say "he was on the floor" with another female nurse. He wore uniforms at that time that consisted of a nylon zipper top worn over a regular short-sleeved shirt, along with white pants. I dutifully ironed both of the shirts and the pants for him before each shift. Thankfully, he worked ten-hour shifts; thus, ironing was needed for only four days a week. Then he went to five days a week as an educator. More ironing. The next hospital educator position required long-sleeved shirts and dress pants. Ugh! At least I didn't have to iron his ties.

Early in our marriage, I had an artist friend who taught art at the K-8 school where I taught first grade. They added sewing class to her duties. After school she gave me some sewing tips. My folks had moved away, taking the machine with them for my younger sister's use. Wasn't that rude of them?

Over the summer, the machines at the school sat unused, so I asked the school if they would mind if I babysat one for the season. They consented since our home was right next door to the school. My friend helped me learn the ropes for sewing a tablecloth and then a silk blouse. I felt so proud and continued to borrow a machine for the next few summers. That catapulted me into the scheme of sewing.

As newlyweds, we lived in a two-story townhouse, with four connected units sharing the same coin-operated machines. It was great that I didn't have to walk for blocks to do laundry. But now I had a new problem: black widow spiders! One brave neighbor brought out his blow torch to kill the egg sacs forming all around the laundry room. Pest control of sorts. Then we bought our first house. The laundry room was in an outside storage room in the carport. I didn't have to share it, no coins required, and pesticides kept the varmints away.

The refrigerator from the townhouse had to stay with the townhouse when we sold it. The renters at the house we were buying didn't feel like moving their fridge with them, and so they offered to sell it to us for a decent price. We were fine with that arrangement but suspected it would only last a few years. That was all right, because we still hadn't struck it rich.

When our first child was two years old, she was playing in the house while Mommy went to put in a load of laundry. It was morning time, and, fortunately, I was dressed but had only slippers on my feet. Being the good little girl that she was, she made sure that the door to the house was closed and—oh, by the way— locked. Oops! I called to her. She came to the door immediately, and I asked her to unlock the door. She didn't know how to unlock it, so I tried to describe how to turn the little knob. I spoke very distinctly in a little bit louder tone so as to project through the wooden door. She felt like Mommy was yelling at her, and so she got upset and went to her room to go to sleep. Evidently, that was her coping mechanism whenever she wanted to block out anything unpleasant. Her bedroom window blinds were open. I could see that she was safely sound asleep.

What now? This was pre-cell-phone days. My husband worked miles away, but normally I could call and leave a message. Not today. He was attending a conference at a hotel miles away. What to do? My other sister-in-law might be home. She lived on the next block. So down the street I trudged in my slippers. Fortunately, she was home and I called the hotel. They said that they could list his name on a message board to check in with the front desk. There they could relay my plea for help. Finally, it was lunchtime, and he just happened to see his name at a glance. Astounded, he quickly drove home before the next session. After that fiasco, we always left a spare key with someone. Our daughter slept through the whole ordeal, by the way.

She had a tendency to pick up colds and infections, so I tried to keep things clean. Good thing that included toilets. She was observed more than once lining up her tiny Muppet characters on the open toilet seat. Perhaps she was pretending that Kermit and Miss Piggy were honeymooning at Niagara Falls.

For Easter, when she was only seventeen months old, we gave traditional goodies, along with a brand new potty chair. She loved that thing and would carry it from room to room and sit on it (fully clothed) to read her stack of books. From whence would she get such an idea? After a week of doing this, she decided to try it for its intended use. She completely potty trained herself in one week.

We still had to send our daughter to church wearing diapers, because she was too shy to ask where the bathroom was. No one else needed it at that age. One Sunday, they excitedly told us at the nursery that she could talk. We didn't realize that this child who had started putting phrases together at ten months was apparently mute at church. From that point on, she didn't have to wear diapers.

Whether we lived near or far from our common destination, my husband and I usually carpooled. At my first year as a first-grade teacher, we carpooled even without a common destination. He would drop me off at my school on his way to the hospital. He had to leave much earlier than I needed to get to school, so I would wait to put on my makeup at the sink and mirror in my classroom. That year, the custodian witnessed me getting ready so many times while he was vacuuming. I don't know which of us felt more embarrassed. By the next year, we had purchased the house next door to the school, so I didn't have to worry about bringing my makeup bag or missing my ride.

We almost always carpooled to church as we often had the same schedule. At times, one of us would have to be there early or stay late for a meeting or rehearsal. The other one would bring a book or toys along for our toddler and wait it out. We only lived two miles away, but we were very green before it was noble.

Every once in a while, we would make the exception. When our daughter was little, she had repeated ear infections or allergy problems, so we didn't want to put her in the nursery on those weeks. One of us would go to the early service in one car, while the other stayed home to allow our daughter to sleep in. During the short break between services, the one who stayed home came in the other car with our pitiful toddler in the car seat. We traded car keys, and the next parent got to attend the second service, while the first one settled our girl back in at home. One time, we cut the time too close, and the hurried second shift was left at the church with a car but no keys.

Because of late meetings at the hospital, early or late rehearsals at church, or some other complicated schedule, we would take two cars to church on a rare Wednesday night. One particular time, during the years when we lived twenty minutes away from church, we took separate cars. I was already home and was ready for bed. Just as I heard the garage door opening, the phone rang. The volunteer worker was calling to say that she was at the empty campus with our abandoned five-year-old daughter. Shocked, I went to the garage to see that my husband was the only one in the car. He didn't even have a chance to get out of the car when I sent him to rescue the worker as well as our scared child.

At times like that, I wished I could push the playback button to see which one of us miscommunicated. It didn't matter whose fault it was; we both have made our share of mistakes. The situation served to remind us of the importance of effective communication. A marriage relationship magnifies that importance. How much greater is the need to nurture the flow of communication with our Maker who oversees our thoughts, marriages, families, everything!

In Matthew 7:7–8 (NIV) Jesus tells us, "Ask and it will be given to you; seek and you will find; knock and the door will be opened to you. For everyone who asks receives; he who seeks finds; and to him who knocks, the door will be opened."

Sometimes the answer is just that simple.

What do you need to communicate to God?

To your husband?

To your children?

To a friend?

Evaluate your listening skills.

When should you have kept your opinion to yourself?

Passion Faux Pas

Have you ever been guilty of trying to keep up with the Joneses? We have actually lived across the street from the Jones family and next door to the Smiths. Exodus 20:17 (NIV) commands, "You shall not covet your neighbor's house [Jacuzzi]. You shall not covet your neighbor's wife [husband], or his manservant or maidservant [cleaning service], his ox or donkey [Lexus], or anything that belongs to your neighbor [Gucci purse]."

What about trying to keep up with the ideal woman or family image in your head? How about trying to be as wonderful as your Facebook friends and families? In my desire to keep up with my ideal and not to commit a fashion faux pas, I broke the tenth commandment and committed a passion faux pas.

At our first house, we had a central vacuum system original to the house. Twenty-five years later, it needed to be updated, and then it was fabulous. The incredible hose could hook up at either end of the house and extend like an extremely long snake. It scared our little girl whenever I vacuumed. That was probably when she first started the falling asleep routine. Better that than tripping and passing out like I did.

When we were preparing to move from our first house with the central vacuum, I was pregnant with our second child. A friend offered to help with some deep cleaning. She had a beautiful home, so I knew she would do a good job. In my sixth month, I knew I could use some help but was not prepared for the embarrassment. She pulled out the stove to reveal many Cheerios, unidentifiable goo and grime, and ta-da—the long-lost Mrs. Potato Head earring.

At our next home, we didn't have a central vacuum, but we did buy a wonderful newfangled vacuum. It was one of the many items stolen when we were burglarized on the day of Grandma Wellman's funeral. Not very good luck with vacuums, I'm beginning to notice.

We still have the Potato Head couple and the recovered earring for our future grandkids to play with. The Mr. Potato Head glasses haven't held up as well since our son wore them, put them on his stuffed animals, and then put them on our Yorkie as part of a costume one year.

When I was pregnant with our son, my husband surprised me with my very own sewing machine for Christmas. What a life changer! It was for him, too. As he was bringing it home from the store, one of his tires separated at high speed on the freeway. The steel belt whipped up and down, damaging our Blazer before he knew what had happened. Months later, the manufacturer recalled those tires following at least one death. Anyway, my husband and the sewing machine made it home safely.

Near my due date, I began having stronger contractions. It was hard to know if this was "it," because of having an irritable uterus with contractions since six weeks along. My husband was helping his ailing uncle to the doctor and with groceries. This was before my husband carried a pager. He called numerous times to check on me. After twenty-four hours of constant strong nonproductive contractions, I told him not to worry and to take his uncle out to eat. Finally, after he stopped checking in with me, I realized that THIS WAS IT! So, naturally, I bathed our three-year-old daughter, straightened up the already perfect house (it really was), set my hair, called the overnight sitter, had our three-year-old gather the trash, changed my clothes, did my makeup, gave instructions to the sitter, kissed our daughter good-bye, and waited for my husband to come home. After twenty-eight hours of labor, forty-five minutes after getting to the hospital, our son was born. Thankfully, the doctor had preordered the epidural spinal block; otherwise, they would have forgone that necessity.

When we called our daughter to tell her to come see her brother, the sitter didn't bring her immediately. It took about an hour. I wondered why. Come to find out, the sitter thought she should bathe her first. Our daughter was used to being compliant, or she really liked baths. One thing is for sure, she was clean when greeting her baby brother.

Soon after our son was born, there was an outbreak of measles. He was too young to be fully immunized yet, so I pretty much stayed home with him for six months, unless we got the occasional babysitter. We never got a sitter for Sundays, as we didn't want them to miss church on our account. I began to feel like I needed a reason to live or something to do of import. That sounds absolutely ridiculous now. I have demands on me almost constantly and would love to be home with nothing going on but to love on my young children. However, at that time, I decided I needed a sewing project beyond my usual scope to keep me busy.

We needed a new bedspread. Remember Grandma's huge afghan? We had shopped and couldn't find a ready-made one to our taste, so we got a sitter, went to the fabric store, and found just the fabric we desired with the right sheen, colors, and design. I created my own pattern and taught myself how to machine quilt around the flower groupings through the thicknesses of the fabric, the lining, and the loft. After about eight months, I completed the bedspread in time for company in December. My family knew that Mommy had made it, and I felt so proud. The proverbial virtuous woman in verse 22 of Proverbs 31 in the New International Version: "makes coverings for her bed; she is clothed in fine linen and purple." I liked that version better than the King James. I was well on my way to becoming that woman, although I was thankful that my home ec. teacher wasn't there to grade the bedspread.

As a toddler, our daughter had frequent ear infections. She had to wear custom earplugs when swimming. Because of protecting her ears and her eyes in the tub, we bought a gimmick called a "shampoo shade." It fit down over her head, preventing the water from running in her eyes and ears. We got a pink one so that she would like it better. It was oval, with corrugated thick edges of foam projecting out from the center. It was a great help, and we used it for years to keep her happy in the tub. When our son was a hilarious toddler, he wanted to have some fun, too. He was small enough at that time to put the shampoo shade around his waist. He danced around hysterically like a ballerina, and that was his tutu.

I began making annual matching Easter dresses for our daughter and me, and always made her a new birthday dress each year. I always sewed our daughter's outfit for the first day of school until about junior high when fashion became the utmost of considerations. We usually purchased our son's outfits, so I would make him a little something instead.

One of my friends was taking sewing lessons and had me over with the kids for a sewing bee. She told me about a dress she was going to make out of very nice expensive fabric. While cutting out the fabric, she made an unfortunate mistake so she scrapped the whole thing. I was in disbelief.

My passion for sewing got the better of me. My niece wanted a new bath robe for her birthday, and so I made her a pretty pink one. Now the word was out, and everyone had a request. I bit off more than I could chew and had to even turn down a paid job for them. I did make a costume for my niece once. I took her to a fabric warehouse, and she picked out the fabric she wanted for her biblical costume. I was in the middle of cutting and sewing when I got distracted by who knows what, and I accidentally cut through a major piece of the fabric. This project couldn't be scrapped! Somehow, I was able to make it work, and the 3,000 plus people per night at the performances didn't know the difference…but I knew.

Another time, I was sleepy and cut some stitches without realizing that my daughter's T-shirt was also being cut. It was one that her friend had designed for her. What was it doing there, and what had I done? Usually, it is the child having to come clean with the parent and confess instead of the other way around. She was so forgiving.

I found the most gorgeous blouse at store, but they didn't have it in my size. I went to three locations before I found it. I wore it like a queen. I felt like Cleopatra. I was wearing it when I was sewing a project. I had to tear out stitches on the project, and you guessed it—I tore my new shirt. That rip was a reminder that I should never hold anything closer to my heart than the One who created me. I believe it goes, "Thou shalt not covet." One day, I finally parted with the shirt but not with the lesson.

Exodus 20:17: Have you been guilty of breaking the tenth commandment?

What have you been holding too close to your heart?

Treasure Trove

We take great care of the things we treasure. The pursuit of those treasures motivates us. Sometimes God allows events to bring us back into focus, so we can see what we've been valuing and then adjust our alignment. Unfortunately, or fortunately, the process never ends. I've made note of a few of my blurry times.

In the box of childhood memorabilia in the storage room was the little pink bowl from my Suzy Homemaker Oven. The bowl became a part of my daughter's play set. I was so happy that my daughter enjoyed domestic tasks and was determined that her exploration not be limited to only her play dishes and pretending to make tea for her stuffed animals. As soon as she could step on a stepstool, I would tie a child-sized apron on her, and she would "help" Mommy cook and bake. What wonderful experiences we had together with her wearing her undies and an apron, so she wouldn't get batter all over her clothes. You see, I had to keep the laundry to a minimum.

Our son was still in diapers when he used that same stepstool to work in the kitchen. He had to taste everything as he went. I would caution him about eating the raw batter. Taste was the sense that drove him, and he wanted to help because then he got to eat the results. He had taken the story of "The Little Red Hen" seriously. It's the story of a group of animals where only those that had helped in the field and with the food preparation were allowed to partake of the feast. In II Thessalonians 3:10 (NIV), Paul states, "For even when we were with you, we gave you this rule: 'If a man will not work, he shall not eat.'" Which came first, the chicken or Paul?

Some other items in the box of memorabilia were my special doll clothes. Our daughter played with my doll and used those clothes on Colleen. She even dressed up our son in them. As a one-year-old, he thought it was hilarious and loved the joke. At some point, he stopped taking all of his sister's suggestions.

Our daughter is a hybrid of organization. She had a few "iffy" years, but overall she was extremely neat. As a young toddler, she loved to put things away. We would open my husband's sock drawer, and there we might find one of her little presents, as we called them. It might be a half-eaten carrot or leftover Cheerios. Things were always, always put away—just not where we'd like them to go.

I remember the day when I got a bottle of formula ready for our daughter, and she was to bring it with her as we were headed out the door. Where did that bottle go? It was nowhere to be found. I finally made up a new batch and off we went. Days later, I dug deep into the bathroom hamper for clothes for a particular load. What did I find? Yes, the once full bottle, along with some moldy and mildewed clothes. We had to throw away at least one pair of underwear.

That experience, along with others, later prompted me to get the kids their own color-coordinated plastic hampers that were shaped like mini trash cans with lids. I wanted them to gather their own laundry. Sometimes I would still find surprises in there. I recall the comical times when they thought that the hampers made great basketball hoops, wheel barrows, or some other crazy thing.

Our son NEVER gave me any challenges. Okay, maybe I would think that I had this angelic toddler down for his perfect naptime. In reality, he was in his room getting into mischief. He once discovered that he could climb out of his crib, open the closet door, and climb up the shelves to the top shelf to retrieve the basket where I safely kept the diaper pins and other products. Fortunately, he didn't poke out his eyes with the pins or anything like that, but he did paint the room and his face and lips with Desitin. That was the first time I had to call Poison Control for him.

Once we moved him into a big boy's bed, he learned that unlike his crib, he could put things under the bed, and Mommy could not see them. I would search high and low for something and finally give up and buy a new item to replace it. It wasn't so easy when a credit card was the confiscated item. Once, he got my lipstick out of my purse to hide for later. Under the guise of a nap, he painted the wallpaper, his face, and a few other things in a very pretty shade of pink. I not only learned to check on him during naps, but, after a few weeks of hunting for keys and checkbooks, I also finally discovered his hiding place.

It was a weekly event, when the kids were young, to visit the Wellman grandparents. Grandma would go outside and sweep the porch area, so we wouldn't track in the messy debris from the desert trees. Often, when we would arrive, she was still sweeping. Our daughter really loved her great-grandmother and was fascinated by her sweeping. We got her a small purple broom just her size, so she could sweep to her heart's content.

Grocery shopping had always seemed like such a lark to me when I was young. I would incorporate playing store when I would play house. I later realized, after becoming a wife, that grocery shopping could be tedious. Trying to bring the fun back, I made it an experience when I took the children along. I never dreamed of having a sitter for such an event. I had a cushy seat that could strap into the cart and would shop for paper towels first so that the rolls could go on either side of the child to hold them upright. The grocery store was where they learned their colors, expanded their vocabulary, and kept an eagle eye out for exciting new products. They learned all of the names of fruits and vegetables in a place that had them all in one spot.

To help ease the monetary sting of the cash register, I took on the personal challenge of coupon clipping. Our daughter loved to help with that endeavor. I was known teasingly as Coupon Suzie even before Coupon Suzy was featured on TV. We saved countless dollars on our grocery bills through the years.

One day, when they were old enough to be walking around on their own or hanging onto the cart and riding backwards, one of the kids got sick right there in the grocery store. The paper towels were used for more than supports that time. "Clean up on Aisle 3" and no more shopping at that location for a year.

Our daughter had a grocery store play set equipped with a moving conveyor belt and a beeper to "scan" every coded product. She loved to play grocery shopping and then pretend to go home, cook the meal, and serve us at her play table with beautiful pink dishes. Our son enjoyed playing grocery store with her only because of the beeping sound. He much preferred his cars and fire trucks.

Eventually, my coupon clipping became a way of life expanding beyond groceries. We had twice as much fun dining out when our check was half price. I learned to scour for deals and shop at secondhand book stores when the library wouldn't do. We started an account twenty years ago at an upscale consignment store near us. This was a great resource as well as a supplement to holding yard sales.

My modus operandi was to use positive reinforcement. We had a reward system using tradeoffs and earning privileges. If the kids had toys out and they wanted a snack and to watch *Sesame Street* or *I Love Lucy*, my pat answer was to tell them how many things they had to put away in multiples of tens. Maybe watching a show was worth "ten," while an ice cream treat from DQ was worth "thirty." Now, as adults, both the kids confess that at times, depending on their mood and attitude, they put those things away by shoving them under their bed. Perhaps that is a universal trick for children?

The Baker grandparents gave our daughter new sheets for her bed. I don't know why it was that I made her earn opening and using them. Hopefully, she only had to take care of ten things, and she couldn't have shoved them under the bed since I would have noticed that when putting on the new sheets! Anyway, they were like gold to her; the blue and yellow ducks against white made her so happy. A few weeks later, I had the different hampers out ready to do the wash. I hadn't noticed a crayon that had fallen out of the pocket of her purple overalls. The crayon got gathered into the sheets. The crayon went through the washer, and what was much worse was that it went through the dryer. Those beautiful, precious sheets were now tie-dyed of sorts.

Matthew 6:19–21 (NIV) tells us, "Do not store up for yourselves treasures on earth, where moth and rust destroy, and where thieves break in and steal. But store up for yourselves treasures in heaven, where moth and rust do not destroy, and where thieves do not break in and steal. For where your treasure is, there your heart will be also."

What kind of treasures are you storing up?

What kind of legacy do you want to leave behind for your children?

Humiliation to Humility

The Scripture instructs in James 4:10 (NIV) to "Humble yourselves before the Lord." More often than not, we have to be humbled rather than humble ourselves. I learned this the hard way after an event, but the good news was that my daughter learned it the easier way.

I have two aunts who make wonderful pies. As a young adult, I would look at the pies with both admiration and sadness. I could never be the "Bakers" that they were. Finally, I got brave enough to try my hand at pie making in the privacy of our kitchen. First, it was just one or the other: either I made my own filling and bought the crust or I made my crust and bought the filling. Eventually, I learned to do it all. Our favorites were the pies made from fresh peaches from the trees my husband nurtured in our backyard. What a delight—whether baked or fresh with homemade glaze.

At one time, I was part of the children's choir ministry at our local church. We had a program where each month we taught a hymn, including its background. The children were rewarded for memorizing the hymn and a few related facts. Seeking to integrate their learning, I requested that our minister of music include the current hymn in the adult service each week. That was not always an easy feat, depending on the theme of the service. As an incentive, I promised him a home-baked goodie each Sunday that he wove the hymn into the congregational singing.

One week, I baked my most perfect apple pie. I was feeling so proud that I decided to enter the state fair that year. I showed the pie to a few of the choir workers before delivering it. I strutted over to the office building. As I was opening the inner door, I stumbled and fumbled. The pie landed upside down on the carpet. Fortunately, God causes all things to work for His good. You see, our daughter has never forgotten this vivid illustration of how "pride cometh before the fall!" Humble pie.

Proverbs 16:18 (NIV) tells us that "Pride goes before destruction, a haughty spirit before a fall."

Take time to reflect on your attitude. Do you detect a sense of superiority in certain situations?

Piece of the Pie

Do you sometimes want to keep to yourself? Perhaps the fear of being humiliated again restricts your scope and clouds your judgment. I found myself guilty of that very thing. What I came to realize is that the second half of James 4:10 (NIV) changes the outlook. "Humble yourselves before the Lord, **and he will lift you up**." Here's the rest of the story.

One time, our daughter gave a piece of peach pie to one of her friends. This friend was a few years older than I but looked much younger. She was gorgeous, fit, seemed all put together with a great family, and was a great mentor. I admired her greatly, and God helped me not to be jealous as our daughter loved her dearly. I was glad for their healthy relationship. She admitted to our daughter that she had insecurities about pie making. Could her mom help her with that? Who? Me?

So, after some planning, I got the house in order, stopped hyperventilating, and had her over for a pie-making lesson. I felt it would be like the blind leading the blind. Instead, it went so well. What a great memory that I can treasure. How wonderful to get to know her better when I swallowed my pride and insecurities. That an experience I'm glad I didn't forfeit.

Pie Maker

By Suzanne A. Fridenmaker

There once was a young woman
who made wonderful pies:

They were spectacular, but not perfect,
tho' she would try.

All the people in town were
hungering for a taste,

The smell would waft and call to them,
but the pies went to waste.

If she cut into here pies,
the beauty would be spoiled,

So she continued to aim for
perfection as she toiled.

One day she realized
Her baking she really should share:

Could the pies be good enough?
Would they like them? Should she dare?

When she shared them...they cheered!
Joy welled up to the surface:

The pies and the pie maker
Had now fulfilled their purpose!

**(Written on April 29, 2004, after the experience
of making pies with our daughter's friend.)**

Artistic Differences

Opposites seem to attract. That is fabulous in marriage, as spouses join together to become one, greater than they were as singles. The problem is that opposites seem to clash, too. The very thing that initially drew you together can drive you apart. Determining your strengths and interests while covering for the other's weaknesses makes the most of your union. I'll share one way that my husband enjoys seeing me express my uniqueness in a practical manner that makes his life easier.

As a young girl, I saw myself as an artist. I was good at drawing and won a contest in sixth grade with my piece displayed at an art fair. I continued to take a variety of classes through school, exploring different art mediums. I later learned that the people for whom I loved to make things didn't seem to appreciate art as art. They wanted useful things. I had a very strong practical side, and so I understood their viewpoint, or at least that was my justification.

As a newlywed, I began making crafts for gifts. I started going with my mother-in-law and sister-in-law to ceramics classes. A student would choose what greenware they wanted to clean, and then decide how they wanted to paint or glaze their bisqueware. Everything was of poured molds. I could use my abilities to make honey servers, bathroom sets, cookie jars, etc. This was much better than making or hand throwing blobs of clay art for which I had previously won awards.

That same mentality reigned with my sewing as well. I wanted to make useful things for people: placemats, aprons, Bible covers, burp pads, and baby quilts. Then I took it a step further by making blankies, burp pads, and quilts that were on a smaller scale: for little girls—when they were old enough—to use later on their dolls. I poured my creativity into gifts that we would have had to purchase otherwise.

The phrase I've used countless times to describe my spouse is that "he likes to have all his ducks in a row." As a nineteen-year-old girl, I thought this twenty-three-year-old guy was so "together" and more mature than all the other young men. Three years later, as newlyweds, when we tried to hang pictures, arrange furniture, or purchase art, his "mature ducks" became an irritant. I loved offset, stylish, eye-catching decorating, and he loved symmetry. I decided to appeal to the part of me that loved antiques, order, and class. We found limitless things on which to agree. I could still love the artsy things without surrounding myself with them, just as he could love hot cars without driving them every day. We have managed to create a home that we can both enjoy. I am at a place where I can still appreciate art or styles without lust or regret. We have rented hot cars a few times when we've gone out of town.

Two years ago, it was time for a new car for my husband. Without car seats and kids to factor in, he got to pick out this one. His new gunmetal gray Ford Mustang with great wheels gets terrific gas mileage and makes driving fun for him. Next year, we will be turning our son's room into a studio of some sort. I'll get most of the say in the decorating. These are little perks, but neither of us would take getting our own way over making the other one happy. We've melded together over the years, influencing each other and growing together. This brings deep satisfaction.

My "together" husband has proven to be such a good provider and such a constant in my life. While he has kept his ducks in a row, those other young men are still lost in the bogs duck hunting.

Through the years, my husband and I have learned that we each have our own areas of expertise, interest, and weakness, and by defining our roles in light of our individual strengths, we can soar. We had to be sure to never sacrifice our commitment to God and His Word, to our marriage, or to our children for the sake of pursuing our own agenda.

What are your strengths?

What are your weaknesses?

What are your interests?

Answer those same questions about your husband, or better yet, with him.

Ask God to mesh you together in a way for an optimal outcome.

Cut from the Same Cloth

Did you name your children before they were born? Did you at least have a girl's name and boy's name ready? We even had nicknames picked out for our children. Once our babies grew into active little people, neither of them seemed to fit those nicknames. They had become their own persons.

We want to lay out a pattern for our children's lives and cut them out using the fabric of our own choosing. But if we are smart, we'll just clear the cutting table, give them age-appropriate scissors and an assortment of fabrics, and let them design the life God has in mind for them.

Years ago, our daughter was ready and eager to learn to sew. We began the same way I learned with the use of paper. She did just great on paper, and I could tell she had very good hand-eye coordination. It was harder when she started to sew on fabric. She knew that Mom wasn't grading her, but her own perfectionist instincts took over. We picked out things she would like to make. One was a teddy bear vest kit complete with a little teddy bear that could sit in a pocket. She entered that in the state fair. Though she did find her picky expectations as a drawback to sewing, she didn't mind getting that blue ribbon.

She enjoyed making a music fabric vest that she would wear for going to the symphony or playing in a recital. Later, she made the more advanced "Teddy Bear in a Library" vest, and then she sewed a gingerbread apron complete with a ruffled trim and pockets with gingerbread men buttons on them. Through these experiences, we found one fear to be true: sewing machine needles can be frightening at times.

One of the safer crafts she enjoyed was making potholders with colored bands and the loom. Sadly, the looms of today are breakable plastic instead of the old metal ones. "They don't make 'em like they used to."

From a very young age, our son would ask me to make things for him. It may be something I would have to draw, build, or sew. I would try my best. I made stuffed frogs with googly eyes, scads of drawings for him to color and cut, puppets, giant crayons for his wall décor, bedspreads, and dust ruffles to better conceal his hidden treasures. He would name it, and I would make it—unless he would ask for something that he had seen on TV or at a friend's house, such as a robot, that could only be made in a factory. They might have plastic and metal parts that I could not replicate. He had such confidence in me. He had seen all the factories on *Mr. Rogers' Neighborhood* and *Sesame Street*. Why couldn't Mommy do it? First of many disappointments, my son.

One day, he came to me and asked me to sew him a quiver for his play arrows. I was rather stymied. He told me to just take an old pair of his jeans and cut off one leg. Next, I should sew a circle of denim to make the bottom. The last step was to cut the heavy seams from the other leg, sew them together lengthwise, and attach them to make strap so he could carry the quiver across his chest.

He loved this so much that we had to make him a loin cloth out of leftover brown Ultrasuede cloth from my dress. Oh, don't forget the black ribbon left to me by Grandma Wellman. It was perfect for making a long braid attached to a headband. On his own, he set up a tent of blankets and sheets. We found a moccasin kit with which to surprise him. He ran the humidifier in the tent to make smoke signals and played a cassette of the Indian songs we had learned for Thanksgiving. All the sewing was done like how you might let a young child experience driving a car. He sat on my lap with his hands over mine, as the fabric moved through the machine. Such pride.

Soon, he could look at almost anything and figure out how it was made. We began to give him old unwanted appliances, whether or not they were broken, so that he could take them apart and see for himself what made them work. He had his own little workshop/stash/ junkyard on the side of the house—his own domain where curiosity and discovery could reign.

Take note of your child's interests and bent. Your children are not "cookie-cutter kids." Within reason, give them the avenues and resources that will allow them to thrive as individuals. This requires attentiveness and creativity on your part.

What can you do to affirm your child(ren)'s pursuits?

Cry Until You Laugh

Do you remember giggling so hard that you felt like you couldn't breathe? What a relief when you could finally breathe again, but you felt oddly refreshed. As adults, we may feel the heavy weight of responsibility such that we take life too seriously, never leaving margins in our lives. Children are a blessing when they bring a wake-up call to our priorities and funny bone.

Our children entered sweet breads, cookies, and crafts in past years at the state fair. One particular year, when we were trying out different recipes, we had a family emergency and had to leave the kids alone for two nights. (Don't call CPS on us!) Our daughter was at that time an experienced babysitter for the neighborhood, but not for an overnighter. We alerted all our trusted neighbors to look out for the kids, but there were viruses going around amongst the neighbors, so it was best to keep the kids home. We also were checking in by phone with the kids, although there were no cell phones yet. What could possibly go wrong? They would be so busy trying out the peanut butter cookie recipes for the fair that they wouldn't have time to get into any trouble.

They made several different batches to experiment with taste, texture, and baking time. Mom wasn't there to remind our son to taste only the finished product and not the raw cookie dough. He could not resist. Our daughter was so brave and responsible when the *Salmonella* bacteria got to him. We couldn't make it home until the next day. That was the one and only time I did not put our kids first. That was the last time our son tasted batter containing raw eggs.

It makes me think of a time when I wanted to use a certain angel food cake recipe. I was so eager until I realized that the Bundt pan handed down to us years before that NEVER got used had become garage sale material. Oops…now I needed one. Oh, well, my Pyrex baking pan would be just fine. Then it happened: the explosion! Cake went everywhere in the oven. The Pyrex pan burst and shards flew everywhere. I didn't want the kids to help because of the danger. They did help, though, by taking a photo of the mess and helping me to laugh in the midst of disaster.

Proverbs 17:22 (NIV): "A cheerful heart is good medicine, but a crushed spirit dries up the bones."

Think of a time when you "lost" your sense of humor. How would a cheerful heart have improved your outlook, your attitude, and your next responses in that situation?

Humor Me

No one lists in their dating profile: lacks a sense of humor. Exactly the opposite is attractive. The same is true as a friend or a mom: humor brings people together and lightens the soul.

I hope you have a friend with a sense of adventure, who sees the fun in life. When challenged to despair, I try to be that friend.

When we hosted music recitals, we started small in our home, and, as we grew, we used churches. I kept making cakes for the receptions, sometimes as many as five at a time, in all different shapes and designs. Later, we went for our daughter's college junior and senior recitals. Her university was out of town, so we stayed in a hotel. We were sure to reserve a room with a real kitchen, although minus the oven. I baked the cakes in her small apartment oven, and then transported them to the hotel to frost and decorate the cakes like nobody's business. You should have seen the looks we got when we used the hotel luggage cart to transport the finished masterpieces to the parking garage. We loaded them into our rental car to take back for the reception at the university. Somehow, the cakes all survived long enough for "oohs" and "ahhs" and photo shoots before they were devoured.

I got brave and confident after all these experiences and thought I would make a cake, instead of buying one, for my mom's birthday club. I thought I would use a recipe from my husband's aunt Dollie, who is ninety-two and going strong. The recipe called for a Bundt pan, but it wasn't an angel food cake after all, so I would use metal round pans. So what's the problem? Right? I saw the chocolate zucchini cake rising and rising like Jiffy Pop popcorn. Oh, no—it will be fine. I just let it make a mess of the oven, since I knew that "no glass would be harmed in the making of the cake." Well, after it cooled and I was able to take what was usable from the baked remains, I decided to cut the overflowing thick monster cakes into more layers. I used a beautiful crystal glass bowl and made the creation into a layered truffle of cake and frosting. I shaped it with a dome, and it looked just like a giant cupcake. Believe me, frosting covers a multitude of sins. The ladies were impressed, even the lady who is a professional cake decorator. I pulled it off and smiled while laughing inside, picturing the scene earlier in my kitchen.

I never did enter a cake or a pie in the fair. That would have been the "frosting on the cake" or a "slice of heaven," but I stayed away from that challenge just in case my home ec. teacher's clone was a judge.

King Solomon also said in Proverbs 15:30 (NIV) that "A cheerful look brings joy to the heart, and good news gives health to the bones."

My children had taught me this lesson so well that when they were not around to make me laugh, I visualized them laughing, and I was able to bring about a good outcome with the "giant cupcake."

Look for ways to laugh in the face of the unexpected and see what surprising delights can come about.

Who's the Boss?

When you work at home, you can easily lose sight of what is important. Everything seems to call for your attention all at once. You might find yourself torn and worn in your pursuits. Haste can make waste, and sometimes it seems like you are shooting yourself in the foot. I can write about these struggles, since I've already dealt with damage control and gone through physical therapy after the shooting. I hope you will learn from my mistakes and come out unscathed.

My sister-in-law Sandy was a great homemaker, and I was humbled after my own kids went through spilled formula and squashed bananas. But I was still annoyed that she let their dog up on the kitchen table, so he could look out the window. How uncouth. It became impulse for me to wash off the table first thing when we went to their house and had to use the table. Years after my sister-in-law went to heaven, we got our Yorkie puppy. He would, of course, stay only in the family room and be well mannered. He soon discovered that he could jump onto the couch, scramble to the back of the couch, climb on the ledge between the family room and kitchen, leap to the back of the kitchen chair, and finally land on the kitchen table. One day, he even figured out how to make it to the counter on the other side of the kitchen and licked the frosting clean off a cake. In disbelief, we accused our young son at first, but then we saw the puppy's beard. We tried to keep the table pushed over and never leave the chairs pulled out. I would smile upward at Sandy every time our dog would make his way to the table.

We often had leftover cake or goodies from recitals that we could not leave out for our Yorkie to get into. A form of "pest control" was to put them in the cool oven out of the way. Whenever we would preheat the oven for any reason, we knew to look first to see if anything needed to be removed. Unusual, I know, but that was our system. I don't recall ever forgetting to check first (whew!), but on more than one occasion, we experienced the "out-of-sight, out-of-mind" phenomenon. Days later, we would find a rock hard inedible "has-been" of a cake.

Once, when my parents were visiting from out of town for Thanksgiving, they would be staying with us. We had worked for days preparing for their early arrival the Monday preceding the holiday. The house was perfect. Over the weekend, we went out for a meal so as not to mess up the house. Food poisoning put a crimp in our plans. We contaminated all three bathrooms and every towel and sheet in the house. I was trying to begin damage control by washing the dirtied linens when the upstairs toilet overflowed downstairs directly above the laundry room. Yuk! My parents stayed at a motel for the first two nights.

Two of my expert Baker aunts and my uncles came to our house in 2004 for dinner. I felt nervous, although I had just gotten a new stove/oven with a flat glass cooktop. I finally had "arrived," because the one aunt had owned one for years. I thought lasagna would be a good choice for dinner as I had made that dish before, although not too often as it was time-consuming. What I didn't take into account was getting used to my brand-new oven. Disaster struck. One of the two dishes turned out horribly, and I had to piece the servings together. How embarrassing. My aunts were kind and understanding, but it took me a long time to recover.

I remember going to my aunt and uncle's home in New York to check out a potential college choice for our daughter. My aunt was almost eighty years old at that time. She prepared the upstairs guestrooms for us, running up and down those stairs to settle us in. Also, she cooked scrumptious meals for us, even checking on the menu with us in advance. I can hardly imagine pulling that off now for my guests at my age of fifty-five. AMAZING!

Later in 2009, both of those aunts came for my dad's eightieth birthday celebration. I made sure I knew what I was doing, and I was used to the oven by then. The meal turned out so well. I asked everyone to move to the living room for music and more celebration. As we got seated, I saw—to my horror—that our Yorkie was up on the dining room table and was licking clean the chocolate remains from the crystal dessert goblets.

Our next meal would be at a restaurant with no cooking and no dog. Perfect. We arrived to be sure the banquet room was ready. We waited and waited. My family was always punctual. Where were they? I had assumed they would come to the same location where we had dined for years with my parents. Instead, my dad picked them up and took them to the location near to the hotel where they were staying. All was forgiven forty-five minutes later, but I can't say that I pulled off even one uneventful meal for my aunts and uncles.

When I got my glass-top stove, I began using the unused burner space for extra counter space when cooking. I might have the seasonings or a bowl sitting on the cold burners so they would be handy. One day, I turned on the burner to heat a large pot of water. I had time to check the washer while it heated. Oops! I turned on the wrong burner, and my plastic colander melted and adhered to the burner. Another time, I was transferring something to a plastic container when the doorbell rang. I set the container down on a burner that had not yet cooled. Haste made waste.

One would think I would have learned from those experiences, bright as I am. The best was yet to come. I had canola oil in a plastic bottle sitting next to the frying pan, in case I needed to add more. I turned the burner on and heard the buzz of the dryer. Wait for it…Wait for it…The plastic melted, causing the oil to leak out and burst into flames. I don't recall my immediate response, but I do remember spending hours cleaning up and airing out the house. Did you know that melted plastic smells horrid and produces caustic fumes? All of these blunders were for the sake of efficiency. Ha!

When I was homeschooling the kids, we had a classroom in our house. Often, we would overflow the various schooling activities into the family room or kitchen. One day, I needed to get the downstairs mopped for music students who were coming later. I asked the kids to keep working in the classroom on their assignments while Mommy "took a break" and did the mopping. Our son, quite young at the time, soon forgot why he should stay in the carpeted classroom. He had on his flip-flops and—whoops!—down he went, catching his jaw on the sharp corner of the coffee table. Now the clean floor was splattered with blood. No stitches were required this time, but we had to go to the dentist. Real time saver. He was okay, except for the calcification on his chin that remained for the next eighteen months.

Colossians 3:23–24 (NIV) says, "Whatever you do, work at it with all your heart, as working for the Lord, not for men, since you know that you will receive an inheritance from the Lord as a reward. It is the Lord Christ you are serving."

It is very easy to get distracted and find yourself trying to do it all and be all and please all. In that pursuit, we often focus on meaningless tasks and lose sight of the big picture. We often end up wasting time and effort when our original goal was efficiency. The original goal must shift to working with our whole heart as unto the Lord. This pursuit brings true meaning!

Evaluate your past motives. What will your renewed focus look like in your everyday home life?

Don't Make a Stink About It

How do you react when things don't go as planned? Do you immediately put up your "skunk defense"? Skunks are cute, but I don't know of any that are welcome in my house.

I have learned that I can't always control what goes on in my household, but I am responsible for controlling my reactions. See if any of these situations smell familiar to you.

Our next laundry room was a room off the family room. It was just great. One day, the machine broke mid-cycle and decided that our family room tile needed mopping. Fortunately, we were home. It seemed to take hours of clean up. The furniture and electronics survived, unlike my stamina! Our young son was so sad to see the machine go. We didn't let him have it in his junkyard. I remember taking a photo of him on top of it with him saying good-bye to the washer.

I flashed back to when he had colic, and I'd put him in a baby carrier on top of the washer to calm him. It was a wonder that he didn't vibrate off the machine. At some point, I decided that putting his carrier on the floor by the running machines was good enough.

Our daughter began her journey with washers when she went away to college. It seemed at first that I got a weekly call about laundry issues. I thought I had prepared her, but then again, look at my record. Dorms, apartments, and then a small rental house later, where she didn't have to share or insert coins, she was all set. The laundry closet doubled as a storage area for infrequently used items, such as the artificial Christmas tree and wrapping paper.

On one special occasion, we flew into town to hear one of her concerts as a professional musician. Ahhh…no cakes, no responsibilities, but she did ask that we come early to help with setup. Piece of cake. She didn't even want to see us before the afternoon recital so she could mentally prepare. Fine. We had the tough job of relaxing in our hotel.

Then it came—the frantic phone call. "Mom, I thought I had some extra time so I put in a load of wash. The hose came loose and drained all over the bamboo floors!" She had used all of her available towels to mop up the mess. Now, she was stressed, running behind, and had a heap of wet towels. Could I help? Our hotel had washers and dryers down the hall for the guests. I retrieved her two loads of wet towels and came back to the hotel. I thought, *Well, at least I won't be doing any cooking.* However, because of unforeseen circumstances for the reception, my husband and I ended up doing food prep, lots of dishes, and clean up. Vacation—yeah! Just like home.

While living in the campus apartment where I had baked the cakes, our daughter had no dog but did have limited counter space, so we pulled the same storage trick for the leftover cakes. I'm not saying who forgot to look, but what a melted mess we discovered when we opened the oven door to put in dinner.

A few years later, when she was in her first rental house, she hosted a recital at a church for her students. Very limited counter space still at this house for the leftover goodies. Yes, you guessed it right. Let me just say that I was not in town for that event. She did find that her smoke detector worked very well.

Her refrigerator was so tiny there. Every time you needed something, you had to take out five things just to get to what you wanted. Then after putting things back in, you had to quickly close the door before an avalanche occurred.

Our son kept asking when we were going to get a new refrigerator like so many other people had. My answer was always, "When that thing dies and not before." Well, we still haven't struck it rich, but we certainly could afford a new fridge. I just wanted to get our money's worth out of that thing! After thirty years, the seal on the door would no longer work even though it still ran just fine. I gave in about a year ago and we upgraded. Woo-hoo!

When my parents were downsizing, they offered the old oak icebox from the cabin. I happily accepted and have future plans for refinishing it. One year, I was trying to come up with a creative photo of our dog for a calendar contest. Our Yorkie was so adorable in the icebox with his paws and head hanging out. It oddly reminded me of the clothes chute. No, he didn't win the contest, but they had all the photo entries on a collage page of the calendar. You can see him if you use a magnifying glass.

Recently, there was the time when our son was trying to design his laundry room for the house he was renovating. The washer and dryer had been outside just under the eaves for decades. I went back and forth with the measuring tape to see the dimensions for reference for the size of the new ones in their future home. He said, "Forget the measuring tape." He simply picked up the dryer, carried it the length of the yard, and placed it in the prospective laundry room. As my jaw was dropping open, I noticed that in moving the dryer, he had disturbed a giant lizard's refuge and a scorpion's nest. Exterminator please!

He was feeling like it would be a while before he could afford new appliances. Oh, well, we live two miles from his future home, and he could continue to wash his clothes (or I would) at our house for the next year. However, it pays to be friendly with the new neighbors. A family was getting a new set of appliances. They told him that if he wanted their not-so-old ones, all he had to do was go next door and get them. He stooped to the use of a hand truck this time. The dryer was great. The washer "may have a leak," he was warned. "I can fix that," he said. He probably can. He has fixed my dryer at least three times. But this is a washer, remember, BEWARE!

He was also redesigning the bathrooms and creating a new one. What a hoot to see him carrying toilets out of the house and setting them in the trash pile on the side of his house. I suspect that by now he knows how they work. Grandma keeps asking when he might be moving in. My pat answer is, "Not until he has his toilets in!"

He opted for an oversized amazing shower instead of a tub with a shower. It is crazy to think back now to the crazy shampoo shade antics. With his muscles and his build, he wouldn't be able to fit it over his hand, let alone his waist.

There was a perfectly good refrigerator in his house. It was filled with condiments and other food when he got possession of his new home. Fortunately, I emptied it out and wiped things down. He was planning on replacing the refrigerator originally but has since decided to keep it till it dies or he strikes it rich. Good thing it isn't filled with putrid food, and good thing it stayed plugged in.

Have you ever been around someone who reeked like the refrigerator could have?

Have you ever had a stench that may have offended others?

"Perfume and incense bring joy to the heart, and the pleasantness of one's friend springs from his earnest counsel." — Proverbs 27:9 (NIV)

Think of a friend who is sweet smelling to your soul.

How can you be the kind of friend who leaves a trail of sweet fragrance?

Wonder Why, Wonder Woman

Do you hold yourself up to a higher standard than that of your peers? It may be at a subconscious level. Perhaps you are seeking approval, or you do not want any finger pointing in your direction. I felt justified in my efforts, but the results spoke otherwise.

I was determined to be Supermom Suzie Homemaker like no other. For years and years, I would stay up late with laundry and sewing, and then turn around the next day and get up early to clean, cook, homeschool our kids, in addition to leading children's choirs, retreats, and field trips for church. Ball games, swim lessons, music students, adult choir, and multiple orchestras topped off the list. I could do it all, I thought. My body decided otherwise.

In 1996, I was getting ready to go to a twenty-year school reunion. I wanted to look great, so I added walking forty-five minutes a day, four to five days a week, and swimming a couple of times a week to my routine. I did look great (I took a poll at the reunion), but I noticed that I had to take a nap that day before the big dinner. That was not my speed. Then we went on a vacation, and I took a nap every day. The family teased me, but I thought I was just making the most of my time off.

Within weeks, I was unable to walk as far as the mailbox. The doctor said that I had two viruses going on at the same time, and that I hadn't slowed down enough. Even though I had rested in between laundry and dishes, I was now on bed rest. No improvement still with this treatment for post-viral syndrome. Finally, after months of testing, with the process of elimination, I was diagnosed with chronic fatigue syndrome.

Through the years, it progressed to include arthritis and osteopenia. What a mess. I had to screech on the brakes and lower my expectations. I still kept busy but had to go on medication and take long daily naps. If I didn't want to keep sleeping until dinner, I would have to set an alarm or we would go hungry.

The kids had to make adjustments, because they no longer had Supermom. I chuckle to realize that in my diminished state, I was probably accomplishing about as much as most human moms. I was just glad to keep the household going. No more regular entertaining to speak of. No more aghast expressions at the presence of dirt in our home. I just had to settle and let the dust settle. Actually, I did a lot more than some working people. You know the irritating naïve question, "Do you work or do you stay at home?" My husband always stood up for me for sure. He appreciated all that I did for the family. My role became that of a helper to everyone. But as the kids became adults, and I needed to pull out of activities, I began to have no identity of my own. That was okay…till this year.

I struggled with controlling my weight for decades. "I was trimmer than lots of women my age," I would tell myself. Diet support groups and methods to follow just didn't seem to work like they should. It was a constant battle. One day, my husband—who had been patient with me buying books and joining groups through the years—suggested that I look into a particular book that had come out. I used my birthday money to get it and read it. We decided that I should try it.

We supposedly have eaten healthy overall for decades, but the food industry had tripped us up. We have returned to consuming nothing that is genetically modified. Some people's bodies like mine don't know how to handle unnatural substances; thus, causing inflammation and immune problems. Hmmm… originally, my motives were selfish and limited in scope: just dealing with vanity and weight. God opened up a whole new life of second chances to me through this.

Suddenly, I had energy that didn't come from the caffeine I had used as a crutch from chronic fatigue.

The aches and pains that seemed to be ever present became distant. I began to have the energy again to be Superwoman. No! No! No! I chose to use the energy for the things I needed to do and saved the rest for the things the Lord wanted me to do. I began focusing on the things that would bring Him glory and benefit me, my marriage, and my adult children.

Suzie Homemaker has come a long way. I still love a good cleaning session, hate ironing, enjoy cooking off and on, and certainly don't bake like I used to. I'm off wheat, chocolate, and sugar for now. What's left to bake already? The wonderful thing is that I feel so much better, and I am wiser for it.

The Lord used those years of illness to break me down. I had a sense about five years ago that I should change my diet. My gut would have been happier if I had listened to that gut feeling. I couldn't let go, though. I loved baking and even more so the delight of eating something scrumptious to momentarily relieve my tension and mask my pain. Suddenly, I didn't need to mask any pain. The answer was there all along, but I was just too stubborn to give in and try the diet change.

Are you resisting God's leading in an area of your life?

Have you tried to "go it alone," perhaps without realizing it?

reModEl

by Suzanne A. Fridenmaker

I've always dreamed of having a home of my own
Where friends and family could feel right at home.
The pride and satisfaction would be so great,
How fun it was for me to anticipate!

Now that I have a large and beautiful place,
It may as well be just a bare, empty space:
Though it is filled with an abundance of stuff,
This remarkable house just isn't enough.

Even though this house of mine is so spacious,
It's lacking the one key of being gracious.
How can I make this house into a real home-
So that I can live here and not feel alone?

I live with my husband, my son, and daughter.
But something is missing. What is the matter?
I've wrestled with this question for many days;
And answer finally dawned out of the haze:

The way to make a hoUSE into a real home
Is to USE it for God as if it's not your own.
The use of the hoUSe I won't leave up to US,
I'll not blame my family and make a big fUSs.

Instead I resolve to give the house to God:
The structure, furnishings, and even the sod.
To create a real hoME was all up to ME-
Yielding it first to God is how it should be!

(Written after an "AHA" moment on November 28, 2004.)

Mission Completed

"Well done, thou good and faithful servant," (Matthew 25:21, KJV) are the words we long to hear someday. I won't stop being a mom until I reach heaven, but my role here on earth changes with the seasons of our lives.

Our children are grown, and I now play more of a supporting role. As the credits roll through the years, my name will continue to move toward the bottom of the list. That's okay with me, as I get to step back in admiration. It reminds me of being at a television set house with only three walls. I have the best view, much like that of a doll house.

As a child, I loved my sister's doll house. I was more interested in the doll house, rather than the dolls that went in the home. I got a doll chair that wasn't just plastic. It was a wingback upholstered chair with gold threads. It was in that memorabilia box, too. My life seemed complete for a moment when we bought our set of embossed, upholstered wingback chairs for our living room. They were perfect. I thought of the doll chair when I sat in our chairs.

For the first few years of our marriage before children, there was a miniature store in town. I would also go to the store in Sedona whenever we were there. One time, after children, there was a traveling display of miniatures at a downtown museum. I loved seeing the display, and our daughter loved it, too. I guess I loved the display and miniatures, because you could create the perfect little showroom with no clutter, dirt, fussing babies, or complaining people.

There is that perfection again. Our Yorkie was another of God's way of bursting that bubble. He loved to perch on those wingback chairs. I grew to love seeing him there. Now, I miss him dearly. The chairs have outlived him.

One aspect of being a homemaker is that your work is rarely done. No opportunity for boredom, except for the time I took on making the bedspread. Continual chores provide job security as long as hubby and family are pleased with your job performance. The reviews can be brutal.

Another aspect that I really like about being a homemaker is that I have so many things going at once that all need to be done. On a "normal" day, I have the ability to go from laundry to dishes to cleaning to sorting to e-mails to crafting to cooking without getting too cramped from being in one position for too long. I like that. The variety is a blessing, and my time is flexible, unlike being on an assembly line. To the one who may drop in unexpectedly, it may look like chaos, but I know what is going on and—hopefully—how to wrap things up by the end of the day. Now, if there is a deadline or planned company coming…Yikes! Drop the oxygen masks now!

I can recall years ago, when I was teaching private music lessons and tutoring in our home, there would be a constant stream of people going in and out. I had to keep things picked up, because parents or chauffeurs may be staying in the other room while I taught. My own children had to be on their best behavior so as not to interrupt Mommy while she was teaching. Our daughter and son were incredibly good and had long attention spans. Often, they would babysit or play with siblings of the students who would come along. How could a mom ask for more?

To our delight, our daughter began playing violin at the age of four and piano at five. She herself began teaching when she was just eleven. By the time she was in high school, she took on the piano students who were too advanced for me to teach. At one point, we had over twenty-seven students.

I am unable to keep up that pace now. Our daughter does, however. She teaches more than twenty private music students, keeping her large home in fabulous style with great organization, so that she can teach with a clear mind. Twice a year, she makes handmade gifts for each of her students. She is learning how to juggle that part of her life with the rest of her rehearsals, gigs, and performances while still leaving a margin for mental, emotional, and physical health. As her life evolves, and she may be blessed with a family of her own, she will be light-years ahead of where I was. What the Lord did for me all those years so that now He can help her in turn. It was all worth it! And oh, by the way, one of her toilets is on a throne, she still uses her gingerbread apron every day, a Swiffer Sweeper is always handy, and she has a bigger refrigerator than mine.

Our extremely manly son is in a good place of being self-sufficient. In high school, he worked for a great employer who taught him his business from the inside out. When his boss chose to take a different career path, our son, then a high school junior, very successfully went into business for himself. This gave him valuable experiences and financially got him through a few years, until he entered his chosen profession. He's ready to run his household of one, with hopefully two dogs, as soon as he finishes his house that he's renovating. So far, scorpions, snakes, black widows, wolf spiders or tarantulas (something large and hairy), and camel spiders occupy his home. Maybe I should take up pest control as my new career.

One of our son's favorite group games is Hasbro's *Taboo*. I don't know if he really likes the game, but he sure loves to drive us crazy with the beeper.

I finally understood the "Calgone, take me away!" commercial. I realized there were screaming children and a barking dog in the background, while the mother escaped to the sanctuary of her bathtub. Our water bill went up after that realization.

Rewards of Motherhood

by Suzanne A. Fridenmaker

Ever since my early childhood
I dreamed someday that my child would
Make me feel so complete.
The part I had not realized
Is that your child is in disguise
Your vapor to deplete!

Even with the work and worry
I wouldn't be in a hurry
To try to change the tide.
Yes, we have had our ups and downs
Oodles of smiles and a few frowns
But it's been a great ride.

Now that my kids are nearly grown
I can let out a silent groan
And pause for a brief rest.
Aah…soon comes the wonderful age
When they respect your wisdom sage
I think I'll like that best!

Not because of all I have done
But because of what they've become
I am filled with such joy!
Through them I understand God's plan
'Specially His endless love for man
Thanks to my girl and boy.

(Written on May 31, 2005, after my first Mother's Day since our daughter left for college.)

101

Rest in Peace

My life isn't over yet. I have new aspirations and look forward to the next stage in life. Now, I am equipped with an advantage, though: peace in my soul.

I am grateful for the thirty-three years of married life and the twenty-two that preceded those. My cooking has improved over the years. Our clothes are usually presentable. But my house is not perfect. My goals have shifted. I want to be able to put my head on the pillow at night and know that I was nurturing, met needs, and showed love. After all, love makes a house a home. But perhaps if I made the perfect pie or the most magnificent cake…No, I don't need "a slice of the pie" or to "take the cake." After all, I'm avoiding wheat and sugar.

My maiden name was Suzie Baker. That name sent a subliminal message. Yes, all the "Bakers" were great at it. In some ways, I would rather be a "Wellman," because I like feeling well again. When I got married, my dad jokingly wanted me to keep my maiden name as my middle name. Suzanne Baker Fridenmaker: what a comical mouthful that would have been. No, I kept my middle name of Allene—named after a lady in the Spanish Mission Church in Florida, where my dad pastored and my mom taught. When I was in seventh grade, we went to Florida to visit Allene. She was a great cook and had us in her home for black-eyed peas.

Now my name is Fridenmaker, and there were jokes about how I jumped out of the "Baker's Oven" and into the "Frying Pan." What I love is the true meaning of the German name originally spelled Friedenmacher. It means "peacemaker." My name changed from Suzie Baker Homemaker to Sue Fridenmaker Peacemaker. "Blessed are the peacemakers: for they shall be called the children of God." — Matthew 5:9 (KJV).

I learned the hard way that "A heart at peace gives life to the body, but envy rots the bones," — Proverbs 14:30 (NIV).

What do you need to do to achieve peace in your heart?

Proverbs 17:1 (NIV): "Better a dry crust with peace and quiet than a house full of feasting, with strife."

Don't mistake this verse as an excuse to serve leftovers. Instead, make your aim to provide a peaceful, warm atmosphere of love at home.

Proverbs 16:7 (NIV) says, "When a [wo]man's ways are pleasing to the LORD, he makes even his enemies live at peace with him."

What can you do to "take the edge off" and bring peacefulness in your home?

Blessings of Royalty

In a previous chapter, I spoke of longing to live in a fantasy world where everyone has the Midas touch. As you have read, my life has not been perfect, but I have been perfectly blessed. I can see now that my misadventures were due to my being amiss in striving for perfection.

I was warned at an early age to be more realistic. It took me years of catastrophes, illness, and humbling experiences to get it through my thick head that THE AWE OF STRIVING FOR PERFECTION only brings me PERFECTLY AWFUL STRIFE! I think God had a lesson to teach me. Perfection is not the goal. JOY in the JOURNEY with those you love, and serving the One you love is the key. Once I let go of the perfection—life is much more worth living.

> "I will sing of mercy and judgment:
> unto thee, O LORD, will I sing.
> I will behave myself wisely in a perfect way.
> O when wilt thou come unto me?
> I will walk within my house with a perfect heart."
> — Psalm 101:1–2 (KJV)

The psalmist was not referring to a perfect house, but a heart made perfect through God's redemption. With that understanding, putting on an apron has a whole new meaning for me, and I am embracing my role in a new way. Maybe someday I will begin entertaining again. For now, most of our socializing is at restaurants or during activities. I want our home to be a fortress of solitude in a way. I am no longer Queen of Clean, though I gladly give my husband the role of Prince under the authority of the King of Our Hearts.

I reexamined Proverbs 31. The New International Version of verse 10 uses "noble character" instead of "virtuous." The whole context of the passage changed for me. The virtues were not a set of skills to be honed or credentials that deemed one worthy of the "Homemaker of the Year" award. The emphasis was on the character of the woman and not on her accomplishments. The accomplishments were a by-product of her noble character. Earlier in Proverbs 12:4, King Solomon writes, "A wife of noble character is a husband's crown, but a disgraceful wife is like decay in his bones." I doubt that serving a meal on stoneware instead of china, or that purchasing a readymade garment instead of sewing it would be the "decay in his bones."

To be a crown to your husband instead of a cancer eating away his bones, what can you do to become that wife of "noble character"?

Proverbs 31:10–31

New International Version

"A wife of noble character who can find?
She is worth far more than rubies.

Her husband has full confidence in her
and lacks nothing of value.

She brings him good, not harm, all the days of her life.

She selects wool and flax and works with eager hands.

She is like the merchant ships, bringing her food from afar.

She gets up while it is still dark; she provides food
for her family and portions for her servant girls.

She considers a field and buys it;
out of her earnings she plants a vineyard.

She sets about her work vigorously;
her arms are strong for her tasks.

She sees that her trading is profitable,
and her lamp does not go out at night.

In her hand she holds the distaff and grasps
the spindle with her fingers.

She opens her arms to the poor
and extends her hands to the needy.

When it snows, she has no fear for her household;
for all of them are clothed in scarlet.

She makes coverings for her bed;
she is clothed in fine linen and purple.

Her husband is respected at the city gate,
where he takes his seat among the elders of the land.

She makes linen garments and sells them,
and supplies the merchants with sashes.

She is clothed with strength and dignity;
she can laugh at the days to come.

She speaks with wisdom,
and faithful instruction is on her tongue.

She watches over the affairs of her household
and does not eat the bread of idleness.

Her children arise and call her blessed;
her husband also, and he praises her:

'Many women do noble things, but you surpass them all.'

Charm is deceptive, and beauty is fleeting;
but a woman who fears the LORD is to be praised.

Give her the reward she has earned,
and let her works bring her praise at the city gate."

Picket Fences

What did your dream house look like? As a child, my image was one with a white picket fence. So far, my husband and I have lived in four houses, none of which has had that nostalgic look. The only reason we plan on moving at least once more is for the sake of our knees. We're thinking that a two-story might be challenging down the road.

A picket fence may or may not be a part of that future home. A nonnegotiable feature is security. I want the kind that not even a twelve-foot electrical fence can provide. Only a loving home where Christ resides can make you feel truly secure and happy.

I hear people speak of hospitality as a gift we must use. I have to listen to God's voice prompting me if the occasion arises, so that I won't swirl around into a tizzy any more. My sister-in-law is having a good laugh in heaven at my antics down here on earth. I now see that Sandy had the true gift of hospitality.

My other sister-in-law gave me an apron that is now worn and tattered, but it is my favorite of all. I use homemade potholders that were passed on to me from Grandma Baker. Recipe cards are my own version of "scratch and sniff" splattered with batter. I treasure the "Hot Fudge Sauce" recipe card today as I think of my aunt in heaven.

My home isn't what I envisioned, but it is a vision! The dust bunnies have multiplied like rabbits. No need to trip over the vacuum cord. Now, I pass out in a cold sweat after vacuuming. Our current vacuum has seen a lot of action over the years, including many haircuts, dog grooming, remodeling dust, and creepy-crawly things. It currently houses one of my favorite socks. I think the bag will be its final resting place. I'm not going in for it.

Today, I keep in touch with our daughter through the magic of cell phones. What did we ever do without them? A few times, the other end of the line has gone silent. I wonder what I said that upset her and made her go to sleep.

Now, the fabrics my husband wears for work are a little easier to iron, and starch is not so in vogue. With the current home health company that he owns and runs, I love the hot months of the year, because "the boss" lets him wear short sleeves. Saves on ironing time, which makes the administrative assistant happier.

My husband still loves meatloaf, though we now use ground turkey. Both of the kids have surpassed my cooking skills. Our son's motivation is still hunger driven. Solomon had something to say even about that in Proverbs 16:26 (NIV): "The laborer's appetite works for him; his hunger drives him on."

Someday, I'll get around to refinishing the antique icebox. Hopefully, I'll sew dresses for a future granddaughter or dolly clothes out of the scraps from our matching dresses. Sewing frogs with googly eyes for a grandson would be good enough for me.

Dad is now with the One about whom and for whom he preached. I am grateful for the confidence my dad had in me. Mom is looking forward to joining him someday at that expansive banquet table in heaven. She has given away all of her aprons, knowing she won't be playing hostess up there. Grandma Wellman's days were cut short due to making the enormous masterpiece of an afghan. I'll apologize to her in person someday, and then I'll give Grandma Baker and my aunts a big hug.

Just in case I thought God was finished teaching me lessons about homemaking, my washer broke as I was writing this. It is interesting to have a front-loader full of gallons of water and wet clothes when the pump breaks. The bailing was a backbreaker.

We recently saw the first season on DVD of *Downton Abbey*. I am thankful for my way of life with my husband, and I am so glad that I don't need someone to dress me and wait on me hand and foot. I'll save that for my later years when I'm bundled in my afghan, with a Yorkie in my lap, at the group home with all the other "washed up," "half-baked" Suzy Homemakers. Till then...life is good. God is even better!

"Trust in the LORD with all your heart and lean not on your own understanding; in all your ways acknowledge him, and he will make your paths straight." — Proverbs 3:5–6 (NIV)

Sue's personal version was written in 2000. "God fulfills all of our dreams of picket fences, even though they may run a delightfully different path than we may have planned."

En**joy** your **jo**urne**y** with **joy**!

Epilogue

Proverbs 14:1 (NIV) says, "The wise woman builds her house, but with her own hands the foolish one tears hers down."

I trust that after reading and reflection you have a clearer picture of what it means for you to be a wise woman. If not, you may want to reread the poem at the beginning, "Home Is Where the Heart Is." I speak of starting with a pure heart, something between only God and you.

Ezekiel 36:26 (NIV) promises, "I will give you a new heart and put a new spirit in you; I will remove from you your heart of stone and give you a heart of flesh."

I pray that God will soften your heart and make you "feel at home."

www.ingramcontent.com/pod-product-compliance
Lightning Source LLC
Chambersburg PA
CBHW031517040426
42445CB00009B/268